Life Class

Poems by Michael Yates

Selected and edited
by John Clarke

Nettle Books

Life Class

This book is dedicated to my lovely sons
Dan and Matt

Originally published 2006 by Currock Press

This edition published 2009 by Nettle Books
nettlebooks@hotmail.co.uk

Individual poems © Michael Yates 2000, 2001, 2002, 2003, 2004, 2005. The moral right of the author has been asserted.

This collection © Michael Yates 2009

ISBN: 978-0-9561513-0-8
Classification: Poetry

Front cover *Seated Nude* and back cover *Self-portrait* both by the author

Events and characters in these poems are imaginary. Any similarity to real characters and events is coincidental. Opinions expressed are not necessarily those of the author or publisher.

Introduction
by John Clarke

Imagine, if you will, a post-holocaust scenario with only two human survivors facing the grim realities of their continued existence.

For Michael Yates, in his poem *Survivors*, such survival will revolve around a supply of modest dry white wine, power for a CD player and all the Harry Potter books. Survival can only take place if the two protagonists accept a shared liking for crabmeat.

And there in a nutshell is the essence of Michael Yates' work: minute detail capturing the absurdities and idiosyncrasies of modern life sketched out on the hugest of canvasses depicting the human condition.

Pick through the poems and encounter the wide array of human life: the apparently sane central figure of *Dangerous to Know* who inspects "the machinery of the grass", or *Wired* about the heroine "full of wires" whose mother can only utter medical platitudes as her dreadful state is hinted at in a tortured telephone conversation.

But if you are thinking that Michael Yates always invents characters to make his point, hiding behind dramatic constructions, then read through *Family*, its deeply felt first person account and its stark conclusion, "Death changes nothing, does it?"

Or alternatively, find the poems originating from his spell as Poet in Residence in North Yorkshire where he seizes the opportunity to scrape away the veneer of tourist board spin to examine real lives and real stories.

Do not be fooled by the playfulness in this collection. Michael Yates may well be cutting a dash ("I wear my yellow socks and lace my old suede shoes") but the serious intent, albeit cloaked in metaphor, is not too far submerged ("But the big brown dog walks behind").

Robert Frost defined a poem as something which starts in delight and ends in wisdom. That definition also serves for the task of selecting and editing the poems for this collection.

And given the enormous contribution Michael has made to Yorkshire poetry and his generosity in supporting the efforts of other writers and poets, the task has also been a great honour.

But don't take my word for it. Read this collection for yourself, delight in the careful observation and appreciate the wisdom of the depictions, for reading this book is truly a life class.

John Clarke's poems have been published in *Retort, Raven, Cutting Teeth, Smith's Knoll, Poetry Monthly* and *Asachi*, a Romanian arts magazine, as well as in various children's anthologies. He has had fiction broadcast on BBC radio and articles published in the *Times Educational Supplement* and *The Observer*. He is Assistant Head Teacher at Swinton Community College with responsibility for language development.

Contents

Abiding Love	9
Age Concern	10
Album	11
Arctic Circle	12
The Bedroom at Arles	13
Beermats	14
The Beggar's Bridge	15
Black on Black	17
Body Count	18
Brick Wall at the End of the Lane	19
Charles Waterton	24
Children	26
Citizen Cain	27
City Heat	28
Colin's Dad	29
The Compleat Court Leet	33
Cross Talk	34
Dr Moreau's Other Island	35
Dangerous to Know	36
Daylight	36
A Done Deal	37
The Drink	38
Each Dawn I Die	39
An Episode of Dr Who	42
Extract from the Minutes	43
Family	44
A Famous Five Afternoon	45
The Farmer's Song	46
The Farmer's Wife's Song	46
Fidelman Revisited	48
Fitter Than Fit	49
Friend David	50
Godchild	51
Hairless in Gaza	52
Handbag	53
The House	54
Hover on the Wing	55
The Incomer's Song	56

Jigsaw	56
Ketchup	58
Laura in the Evening	60
The Left Side of My Brain	61
Leonardo	61
Life Class	62
Limestone Pavement	63
Little John: A Political Memoir	64
Love a la Carte	65
Love Strikes	66
Love's Consolation	66
The Maddest Thing	67
Midsummer Nightmare	68
Mostly Unaffected	69
Mystery Play	70
The Naming Game	70
The Neat Goodbye	71
Novelty	72
Number	73
One Day He Pushed the Dinner Plate Away	73
Pet Names	74
Peter the Pathfinder	75
The Planting of the Penny Hedge	77
Poet's Summer	81
Police Presence	82
Portrait of the Artist	83
Preparations	84
Prepared to Make a Statement	85
Psalms and Proverbs	86
Rear View Mirror	87
The Reception	88
Rhymers	89
The Risks of Love	90
Shocking Memories	90
Showstopper	91
Sins of the Fathers	93
Skeletons	93
Skunk Tale	94
Some of Us Make Ourselves Sick with Hope	95

Soulmates	96
The Stephen Joseph Theatre Restaurant	97
Sunset at Helenopolis	98
Survivors	99
Tellyland	100
Those Wayward Boys	101
Travelogue	102
A Trick Worth Knowing	102
Voices of War	103
Wagonwheel	107
The War of the Worlds	108
We've Not Had Much of a Summer So Far	109
What	109
Wired	110
Woof and Warp	111
Words	112

Michael Yates is a graduate of London University. He has worked as a journalist for the *Wakefield Express* series and the *Huddersfield Examiner*, and has written book reviews for the *Bradford Telegraph*, film reviews for the *Sheffield Star* and theatre reviews for the *Yorkshire Evening Post*. He has won the RICS newspaper journalist of the year award for feature writing and was one of the prize-winning team who produced the special edition of the *Sheffield Star* following the Hillsborough disaster.

He has published short stories in magazines and anthologies and has won awards for his stories from the Armagh Writers Festival, the Jersey Arts Centre and the Wolds Words Festival. He has been Poet in Residence in North Yorkshire and Poet in Residence at Wakefield Cathedral and in Wakefield Hospitals. He has had six plays performed by Yorkshire theatre groups in Wakefield, Leeds, Featherstone and Pontefract.

In 1998 he founded Wakefield's Black Horse Poets who still meet regularly for workshops and also hold public readings.

He has taught playwriting at Harrogate Theatre and creative writing in general for the Workers Educational Association.

Various poems in this book have been published previously in book form in *Trust Me, I'm a Poet* (Storyteller, 2000); *Full Gallop* (Storyteller, 2000); *Poetry in Motion*, (Scarborough Council & North Yorkshire Libraries 2000); *Louis and Friends* (Cathedral Poets, 2002); *A Very Special Collection* (Cathedral Poets, 2004); and *Not Dark Yet* (Currock Press, 2005). Other publications in which poems have appeared include *Jigsaw* (CD and booklet, with Marian Walker, Storyteller 2001); *In Balance* magazine (2001); and *Off the Page* (published by Wakefield Libraries, 2003).

Abiding Love

Think me desperate with myself
To be so angry with you,
Or so full of morose abandon.

It is myself
I am fallen out of love with.
It is myself I cannot bear
To bear witness to.
How much harder then
Is the double-image,
Myself and you, intertwined
And feeding off each other.

And don't imagine it's
The years have
Made the difference. No.
It's the *days* that take their toll,
It's the *moments* that imprison.
Our love is infested with words,
Our relentless life
Confirmed in a sentence.

Age Concern

I want no younger men
Taking advantage. I need
No competition from the
Coming generation. Lop off
Their heads, I say. Or poison
Their babyslush. I see no reason
Why they should threaten
Me with their obscene and
Violent joy, their taste for
Things ecstatic and electric,
Their ability to laugh at
Novelty, when my reaction
Is – very sensibly–
Fear and loathing.

See then they confine their casual
Sprawling to the graveyard
And so give me some
Elbow room up here.

Album

Talk is cheap but let's not talk of the devil:
speak his name and he's glad to appear,
only too eager with a tail or two
and a tale or two,
happy to render us the truth,
happy to spread a little hell.

Now there is no love between us,
let us talk of old love instead.
Now there is no common ground,
let us at least avoid the void.
Let us do better than an E for effort
and an F for fail.

Talk is fine but let's not talk philosophy.
We are far too old to have a view
except a *deja* view.
We are too far gone for feelings
except feeling adrift.
Let us recall instead the day trips we've enjoyed.

Now there is no longer emotion between us,
let us talk of others' emotions instead.
Let us mention schoolfriends and bedmates
as if their deaths had not been acts of betrayal.
And, yes, of course we'll do it again next year.
I always say it's something to look forward to.

Arctic Circle

('No light, but rather darkness visible
Served only to discover sights of woe,
Regions of sorrow, doleful shades, where peace
And rest can never dwell, hope never comes'
- Milton's Paradise Lost, Book I)

        when they returned and found they were lost.
And it seemed they stood in the centre of something
                                  distant

inside the heat of snow
seeing streaks of white sky like empty sheets of paper,
everyone asking where did we make a wrong turn
and when did you or you notice? And
why didn't you say something earlier?

There has to be a champion, the white bird strong
                                  enough to fly
out of the trap and camouflaged to escape
                                  surveillance.
They asked for volunteers then took a vote.
I voted for you.

Now they ask why you are not returned with help
and I say you must be having problems
and they should be patient,
and some of them are saying:
The white heat of the snow isn't so bad
if you take off your parka and your snowshoes in
                                  homage,
and I say they should be careful
and watch the sky for your return,
but I no longer believe in myself
and even catch myself no longer believing in you.

And some of them think they have already escaped
while others declare there is nothing to escape from
and Corporal Finnegan has forgotten altogether
that awful moment

The Bedroom at Arles

The first thing you notice is the chair.
No-one could sit there. The care
that went on making it in cakey paint
expresses a different kind of creation, no taint
of relationship or general theme.
The door and hat and bowl are separate, each
                                              self-supreme.
The windows give no view, the light is rendered hard
like ice; a winter scene of frozen summer sun,
                                               a postcard
from the north pole of the heart. Now you see
that every object fights for its existence, struggles free
from drowning in the universal stream, explodes
                                               the heap
to which reality consigns us all. You keep
the bed till last. Its narrowness is sinister; it sings
                                               of pain.
The man who lay there once will never sleep again.

Beermats

The elegance of beermats,
the frank on a Maltese blue.
I shall make myself a collector
now I've lost my collected you.

Miniature bottles in bathrooms
of shower gel and apple shampoo,
programmes from Ayckbourn and Godber
will fill up my life anew.

If it wasn't for the rain
I might go out more.
If it wasn't for the rain,
Bitter pitter-pat.

The gentle hum of the CD Rom,
the slo-mo DVD view.
I might even ride on buses
and collect a ticket or two.

And if it wasn't for the rain,
I might go out more.
If it wasn't for the rain-oh!

Bitter pitter-pat,
Pitter-pat-pat.

The Beggar's Bridge

(Tom Ferries was an Elizabethan adventurer. Penniless, he loved Agnes, the landowner's daughter, but was despised by her father. He would swim across the River Esk to be near her when her father was away. He eventually became a wealthy privateer, plundering Spanish treasure ships, and won her hand in marriage. He then became a successful businessman. When she died, he built a bridge across the Esk in homage, and carved on it his name and the date. What interested me was the curious mixture of pirate and respectable businessman, of devil-may-care lover and builder of 'safe' bridges.)

Every woman wants a pirate,
the cutlass and the grappling irons,
every woman thinks she can tame him,
turn the sinker of ships
into a builder of bridges.

Every woman loves the outsider,
the beggar beyond the gate,
the man with no past
who has to invent the future
to build a bridge to *her*.

A light at the window when her father's away,
and he swims the Esk at Glaisdale,
lies amorously with his love.
A light at the window when her father's away,
a signal to his respectable heart.

Tom Ferries became a pirate,
a career with prospects in those days.
And promotion came as expected,
doubloons and pieces of eight
greatly enhancing his prospects.

Returning as rich as the next man,
he was granted the hand of his Agnes
and lived with her a respectable time
with a nice respectable business
based on his interest in shipping.

A light in her eyes when he comes home at night
smoothes from his brow the cares of the office,
makes him forget the accountant's report.
A light in her eyes when he comes home at night,
a signal to his respectable heart.

When Agnes died, he tore his hair,
he suddenly looked like a pirate again.
For his heart had returned to stone,
and he swore to build a monument
that she might turn to stone too.

And there it is - the Beggar's Bridge,
though it might be called the Pirate's.
And there it is - so people may cross
without getting wet or bothered
in their search for conquest and love.

A light through the trees when evening comes
falls on his name and *1619*.
Nowhere an echo of the clamour on decks,
just a light through the trees when evening comes,
an epitaph to his respectable heart.

Black on black

We philosophise over coffee
while our awkwardness spills into the saucers.
Half a bottle of Bell's ago, I pushed myself past sleep,
and for his sake watched blind night come down.
Now I hear myself say:
 'Hey, hey, hey…
You can do it, you know. You can make it.'

My little brother does his little laugh. He
throws in two more sugars.
No sense trying to keep
him here - he's ratcheted, wound
beyond bearing,
beyond ensnaring.
And I, suddenly sober, am not sure I can take it.

Yet I remember other times,
blacker nights in blacker climes
and gallons of blackest coffee,
before his Lisa left him, before even our Maggie left
me.

And I remember *The Casting of the Runes.*
And fleeing all those demons in the past.
And I remember *Prufrock* and the spoons.
And no - it's coffee *cups* measure out our lives at last.

Body Count

I sing the body eclectic. A little bit of this, a little bit
                                                                         of that.
I sing the soul of discretion on the way to the grave.
I sing the dark soul after midnight and poor souls
                                                 under the sun.

After the verse, the chorus:
Da-dee-da. Da-dee-da-da. Doowah-diddy.

I sing the body politic. A little bit you, a little bit me.
A little bit of devilment. A little bit of a problem.
I sing the dark side of the state: the homely homicide.

After allegation, interrogation:
Da-dee-da. Da-dee-da-da. Doowah-diddy. Dead.

After the violence, the silence.

When I saw John Wayne at the Ramada,
I said: "You don't look so bad
for the man of a hundred gunfights."
He said: "Movie heroes never die.
We live in an age of computers
– even Fred Astaire can still come dancing."
I said: "It's those scientists again.
What will they think of next?"
He said he didn't know. He was just a cowboy
                                                         at heart.

Back in my room, after wide screen and Dolby,
Doo-wah-diddy.
Back in my room, after the silence,
Doo-wah-diddy. Dead.

Brick Wall at the End of the Lane

There's no such thing as pain, no such thing
                                              as sorrow.
That's what Dr Cheever says and he should know.
Dorothy, he says, God doesn't make mistakes,
else he wouldn't be where he is today.

When I was little, I had lots of looker-afters.
And some of them were nice and some of them
                                              were not.
Dr Cheever says forgive them because they tried
                                              their best,
even Mr Crowther who was prosecuted.

And then I was grown up and then I lived with Ian.
One day we sort of met, one day it sort of happened.
Dr Cheever says souls seek their counterparts.
Ian hated his mum so we had a lot to talk about.

I still have good feelings even after the court case.
But I couldn't see it then - I thought he didn't
                                              love me.
Dr Cheever says he loved me but didn't know
                                            how to show it.
I still have the scar on my neck. Look. Here.

I saw a church with a poster *Carpenter needs joiners*.
So I started going regular, having cups of coffee.
That's how I met Julian, the computer engineer.
I was shocked when I found he was married.

There's a brick wall at the end of the lane with lots
                                            of loose bricks.

And so I got a brick and I threw it through
                                            his window.
And I threw the washing off the line and I trampled
                                            it into the lawn.

Life Class

You wouldn't think a man could have so
                                      many underpants.

And I didn't go back to my job
because Julian got it for me.
It was just a crap job.
And I fell behind with the rent and I started
                                      drinking again.

And the people at the church, the people I had
                                      coffee with,
they didn't help at all.
They said Julian never cared for me.
And they said I shouldn't drink.

So I went down to the end of the lane
and I got another brick and I threw it through
                                      their window.
(Oh, it wasn't stained glass or anything
- we don't believe in graven images.)

That's when I went to the doctors
(the *medical* doctors, that is).
And they kept giving me drugs: Ativan, Librium,
                                      Equinol.
Poisons, Dr Cheever says, poisons polluting my soul.

And I had to live in a hostel.
That was rock-bottom, that was the pits.
I felt I had no friends.
But I did have a friend, I just didn't know it.

That's when I saw Dr Cheever, his picture in *Hello*.
It was an advert for Good Life Therapy.
You could get it on the NHS if your GP agreed.
My GP was only too pleased.

Dr Cheever was just like his photograph.
And he told me all about Therapy,

Life Class

how you had to be positive in everything,
see the love lying latent in your life.

And oh, he was just like his photograph!
The colours were so life-like.
He said everyone could believe if only they knew
- but how can they know until they believe?

And straightaway I saw he was right.
And straightaway I booked six hourly sessions.
But later on I tried to book a seventh,
and Dr Cheever said: *Sorry, the NHS only paid
                                                for six.*

I went back to my GP and severely damaged
                                    his stethoscope.
But he said it wasn't his fault.
It's all rules and regulations these days
and I'd have to pay for myself.

I went back to the hostel
and I cried my eyes out.
I could *never* find the money.
I nearly took an Ativan but something inside
                                    me stopped me.

It was something Dr Cheever said.
It wasn't till the morning I remembered.
I was looking at his picture in *Hello*
and the words popped out.

*Everyone can believe if only they know
- but how can they know until they believe?*
So when things seem bad,
it's just another kind of good.

Then I turned the page of *Hello*
and there was this crossword.
And I'm no good at crosswords

but I thought I'd give it a try.

So I borrowed the warden's pencil
and I got six answers in ten minutes flat.
And when I read them backwards, a line of
                              letters spelt LOVE.
(Except for an M and a W.)

And that's when I knew Dr Cheever loved me
- not just the kind of love in Good Life Therapy
but a personal love for me *alone*.
And that's when I knew I loved *him* too.

So I went round to tell him I loved him,
we were two souls seeking our counterparts.
But when I got to the waiting room,
the receptionist wouldn't let me in.

And so I started screaming
and threw an inkwell at the fish tank
and I think it hit the guppy.
And Dr Cheever came out and I told him everything.

He said something about my needing Equinol
but I knew he was only testing.
Then the receptionist called the caretaker
and they bundled me down the stairs.

They said don't come back or we'll call the police.
But I forgave them.
I could see they really loved me
but didn't know how to show it.

Next day I went back again
and there were two men on the door
and they used very bad language
even when I showed them the crossword.

So I had to look through the phone book.

Life Class

There were 17 Cheevers, and ten of them
                               were doctors.
I spoke to nine
before I got mine.

A woman's voice answered.
The voice of the fat receptionist.
And then I understood!
And then I understood everything!

If he was living with that woman,
how could he tell me he loved me?
How could he do it with that very fat woman around?
No wonder he put it in a crossword.

Well, you know the rest. It's in the report.
The phone calls. The letters.
The windows as well.

There's a brick wall at the end of the lane with lots
                                         of loose bricks.

I know he loves me and I know we'll be together.
But you can't know until you believe
- and when you believe, you know.
There's a brick wall at the end of the lane. But
                             you can always climb over it.

Charles Waterton

...born in 1782, was an explorer, naturalist and passionate Catholic, and maybe also a liar. Born at Walton Hall in Wakefield, he nearly died of yellow fever in Spain; in Guiana, he managed plantations, dissected animals and carried out diplomatic missions; in the US, he fell in love; in the Netherlands he married someone else. He returned to Walton Hall where he established a sanctuary for exotic animals. His wife gave birth to a son but then died. Waterton's obsession was making mythical monsters out of animal parts for a sort of rogue's gallery of the people he hated - mostly Protestants. He also created the Nondescript, a monkey which he made to resemble a customs officer who had once insulted him.

I.

Son of the Squire and son of the Jesuits,
climber of trees and chimneys,
I rode to hounds and jumped over Yorkshire hedges.

(And always the drumming of the hunters' hooves!
I look across the field for something else.)

In Spain, I spew black vomit
(*vomito negro*, I was learning the language)
in plague city where my uncles died.

(And always the drumming at the funerals!
I look round for a ship.)

In Guiana, I rule over sugar cane and slaves,
killing and dissecting unknown snakes,
riding a crocodile in the raging Orinoco.

(And always after, rush of water in my ears!
I look for something dryer.)

Over great oceans, carrying intelligence,

Life Class

sealed orders from potentates, entreaties
                          from emperors,
I know myself to be worthy of trust.

(But often the drumming of my fingers on the desk!
I look for myself and see the hired man.)

Washing my feet in Niagara Falls
I fall in love unrequitedly
and make no further mention of the lady involved.

(And always after, a lesion in my heart!
I begin to look for home.)

II.

In Bruges I marry and in Wakefield she dies,
giving birth to my son while I make the Nondescript
out of two howler monkeys and a tax inspector.
I build a wall round Walton Hall,
a place, you see, for my menagerie.

Outside I leave
a few books and letters, unbelieved;
a few creatures catalogued, unremembered;
a few messages brought, but no reply.

Inside I give
mud to my reptiles,
river to my fish,
sky to my birds,
and prison to mine enemies.

From gorilla face and donkeys' ears, that's
                          Martin Luther.
From lizard tail and batskin, Bad Queen Bess.
Rhesus hide and dogshead are Darwin's evolution.
And inside each of them an emptiness.
And in each of them myself.

Children

In the dark I dreamed
my children no longer loved me.

My black-haired son turned his leather jacketed back
while my honey-freckled daughter shook her candy-floss
head decidedly.

It was growing-up that had done it, they said.
I had not turned out as expected.

Now they re-write the backlog of their lives
in the electric light of new knowledge.
For outlived affections must never be recorded
lest they embarrass the grown-ups
by turning up at family parties
like 8-mm movies
of bath-time and potty-training…

So I awoke with a start,
sweating and cold,
in the bed of their mother.
But when I tried to call out,
I could not pronounce her name.

Let bright morning come and change all this.
Let bright morning tell me: in this dark I *still* dream.

Citizen Cain

If there was any way
To end this without blood, I
Didn't know it.
I went at him.
He stuck a knee in my
Balls. I yelled and rolled and
Bit his nose. He
Fell on me, his hands
Around my throat. The
Pulse throbbed in my head, turned
Scarlet in my eye. Then I
Rolled again, came out
On top and banged his head
On the bare baked earth, took
A smoothly-rounded stone and hit him hard.

He subsided.

Afterwards I hid the body but
The Lord God knows everything
– God damn it! –
And he came at me at
Evening, looked at me with
Hooded eyes and holy rage.

I tried to talk of passive violence,
How my brother's attitude provoked.
But all the same I suffered
– exile, terror, the brand on the face.
So Abel had won. God
Grind his passive bones!

I will not subside.

City Heat

A shame that nature means nothing to me
Shades to the blind man
Symphonies to the doorpost
Because otherwise
I could soar on silver birdwings
Or shake the symmetry of oakleaves.

Since nature means nothing to me,
Reduced to a steel and plastic life,
I embrace the ground-level glance,
Those shoe-leather treks and bus-ticket odysseys.

And I'm resigned to be
Preserved, if at all, in concrete.

Colin's Dad

I CAN'T believe they'd treat us
like this, people we've known all us lives,
people who'd see us down club and greet us.
But when it comes to brass, the knives
come out. I'm so fuckin mad.
I *am* Colin's dad.

They say Jimmy Street, Colin's so-called friend,
got eight grand from *The People*. But Kevin Strong
- he's our solicitor - reckons in the end
(and he's not often wrong!)
it was more
like four.

Kevin Fuckin Clever Strong says I could have
                                        had *twenty*.
But I made the mistake
of not going to the *Mail*. We'd got plenty
of holiday snaps, school reports. I *ache*
to think what we've missed, Colin's mum and me,
when others who know nowt have had a ride for free.

Colin's mum, our Kath, would do anything I say.
Not like that Rose, that slut our Colin wed.
She kidded him there were a kid ont' way,
Oh, don't you know, she just led
him on.
Now she gets paid to tell lies to *The Sun*!

The worst of them all to my way of thought
is that Mr Ferris, Colin's old teacher.
Mr *Ferret* is what the kids call him. There ought
to be a law, like with a preacher,
a doctor or owt,
to stop them go blabbing the whole show about.

Life Class

He said in *The Mirror* our Colin was a lonely kid,
with not many friends and not very bright.
Who knows the harm that sort of thing did?
Not very bright! Now is it right
that a teacher like him can get away with libel?

You don't need a lawyer to see that it's liable
 to hurt Colin's prospects in later life,
(this libel's a funny old business, mind!)
spreading lies like that, making rumours rife.
There were lots of unkind
things said about me, some nasty stuff.
And I told Kevin Fuckin: *I've had fuckin enough*!

They said I beat Colin when he were a lad,
                                took a strap
to our Kath. But that was hear-say, all second-hand.
Now show me the man that hasn't given a slap
to his wife when she's mithered him, raised a hand
to his child for chastisement. It's sad
but it's just part of being a dad.

The night the police phoned us up, Kath and me,
it didn't look so bad
as far as we could see.
After all, Colin's just a lad,
it wasn't the end of the world,
it was just this *girl*.

She was probably on drugs and stuff
and he'd gone a bit too far.
So she couldn't take a bit of rough.
Well, you know what young lads are.
And whose fault is it then?
You can't blame the men.

Then they told us the rest.
Said he'd confessed.
Four.

Life Class

No more.
Told us dates and places.
Pontefract fair, Doncaster races.
Bits of hair and skin, DNA traces.
I told him: Say nowt!
He said: Too late! It's out!
Four lives.
One screwdriver, three Stanley knives.

So what I'm telling Kath is: we've got to bring
our minds to bear,
make the best of things,
get a share
of what's about.
It'll all help Colin when he's out.

Four life sentences? What's it mean?
I know a bloke killed his wife and three kids
and ended up in Winson Green.
That's four in all, same as Colin did,
and he was out, no fear,
after 13 year.

And our Colin's still young.
He'll still have a life
when his time's done,
get a new wife,
have those grandkids that Kath talks about,
have a good time when he's finally out.
But Kevin Fuckin Clever shook his fuckin
                                                clever head.
Don't count on it, he said.

Still, it's an ill wind that blows
- and some of the victims' mums
are planning to sue our Rose
for Colin's house and some of the crumbs.
That means she could get took
for all the money from *her* new book.

I'm inclined to give her a bell some time,
offer a way to protect her profit.
After all, *we've* committed no crime,
we should be allowed to cream something off it.
I'll suggest a deal so her publisher could
do us *both* some good.

But I can't believe they'd treat us
like this, people we've known all us lives,
people who'd see us down club and greet us.
When it comes to brass, the knives
come out. I'm so fuckin mad.

When all's said and done, I *am* Colin's dad.

The Compleat Court Leet

The Court Leet in North Yorkshire dates from Saxon times and can still fine people for grazing too many sheep on common land, letting rams out too early in the season, stealing peat and so on - though I understand the fines tend to be on the small side.

At Danby
let a man be
brought to us
in court to us
and plead his case,
admit disgrace,
as in ancient times was meet.
For we are the Court Leet.

Since the time of Tancred the Fleming
our well-wrought judgements on hemming
in sheep are paramount:
it is we who rightly count
just how many should graze,
and for just how many days.
Do not think it mere conceit:
for we are the Court Leet.

And when it comes to rams, sir,
it is we who hold the answer.
We name the date. See you remember:
not before November
shall ewe be turned to dam
and produce a healthy lamb,
so it may safely bleat,
courtesy of the wise Court Leet.

Deception will be no avail if
we once send out our bailiff
to pursue the miscreant.
Though information be scant,
we will skewer him to the hilt

for the wall he illegally built.
Let no man think to defeat
the righteous judgement of the Court Leet.

And though our fines mere pennies might yield,
and though our power be restricted to field,
and though we meet but once a year
and though we are old, still have a care
that you obey our laws, sir.
We've been here since before Chaucer.
And that has proved no mean feat
for a body like the Court Leet.

Cross Talk

As Jesus always has to be guessed at,
either turning the other cheek or turning over the
                                      moneylenders,
here is my guess at Him
(that's Him with a Capital Aitch).

He is as much the brother of Moses
as he is the son of God.
But He is the Younger End of the family,
the Radical Rebellious One with the haircut.

And when Paul kidnapped Him,
forcing His followers to be drinkers of blood,
a strange thing happened:
Jesus did not take well to being Cut Off.

He had always needed his Caiaphas
and later his Constantine.
He had to mix with money-gold, blood-red,
                legal-black and politic-purple,
if only to offset a life-in-death pallor.

Then Francis and Dominic re-enacted the scheme
in their middle age,
the one living like a Lord,
the other living out the Law;

the first still fishing for men
and trusting to word of mouth;
the second finding illumination
in a manuscript.

The prism and the schism:
if Jesus is a colour in the spectrum coat of Joseph
and the garment is rent asunder,
there is bound to be gnashing of teeth

and usually spilling of guts.
A pity He had to be a Carpenter then
instead of a Tailor;
sawing us apart instead of sewing us together.

Dr Moreau's Other Island

When two deaf lesbians from America
want a baby as deaf as they are,
they have a world of technology waiting:
computerised genealogies to identify a donor
and a sterile disposable syringe for the practical bit.

Whereas the poorest beggars of Bombay,
if they want to smash the legs of their offspring
to maximise success in a competitive business,
have to rely on old-fashioned sledge hammers.
Now what I say is this: *Is that justice?*

Though I suppose it shows
traditional methods still have their place.

Dangerous to Know

He wandered into the lounge bar at two
And bought a half of shandy.
He saw faces in the wallpaper leering,
Eyes in the stained glass window staring;
Hands chiselled on table legs
Clenched into fists.

He caught the bus to the park
To eat his egg-mayo sandwich,
Inspected the machinery of the grass,
Cogwheels among the tree roots.
He caught the nervous whine of
Engines in the wind.

He had one consolation:
Only *he* could see how things really worked.
And he knew that made him
Dangerous to know.

Daylight

Friends gone, bottles
Emptied, thoughts turned inward.
Was it this cold when we started? No.
Nor so late we couldn't find
Comfort. But the dawn brings
Harsh light, the pillow is wet
With alcohol sweat. Tentative
Birdsong is the hum of habit
Over joy. Memory invades
So I am reminded that
My time with you is irrevocable,
Though you lie in your half of the bed
Unconscious of it all. You
Sleep, I wake, I'm
Turned inward, turned away.

A Done Deal

The spoons have it.
They glitter beneath the table lamp,
More useful than the forks
Who have no talent for liquids,
Less scary than the knives
Who like to be thought of as sharp.

"The spoons have it," I say to my companion
and top up her glass.

She smiles like a spoon
As the waiter hurries over with the bill
Inclusive of St Emilion and VAT.

In the hotel,
Once business is concluded,
She spends eight minutes in the bathroom
And I watch the Midnight Movie.

Cary Grant is as suave as ever.

When reception rings to announce the taxi,
She waves a vacant hand
And edges out into the hall.

I am left with Cary on the plasma screen.
He glows like the brightest spoon of all.

The Drink

Where the boat stops, there stop I
with the Black Horse Tavern nigh
under a bold and restless sky,
weekend adventuring.

When the boat moves, then move I
from the Black Horse by and by
under a pale and loitering sky,
lounge bar adventuring.

In the drink
boat float.
In the drink
I think
I sink.

When the boat rocks, then rock I,
to and fro, do or die.
In the cabin puce I lie,
adventuring postponed.

Each Dawn I Die

...is the title of a film in which George Raft gives himself up to the cops to save the life of his friend James Cagney. In fact, Raft and Cagney were friends in real life though Raft was also the friend of gangsters while Cagney was a campaigner against organised crime in Hollywood. One day Raft discovered his mobster friends were planning to kill Cagney and he put his own life at risk to stop them. So life, as always, imitates art.

Jimmy Cagney took the rap but they *put* him in
                                                                the frame.
He was wild-eyed and innocent, bad acting his
                                                                only shame.
This time he didn't do it but the judges couldn't see
He was going down to Sing Sing for the likes of
                                                              you and me.
The Mob stole the car and kicked him all about,
And over Jimmy Cagney they poured the whisky out.
When he woke up in the wreck, they said he'd killed
                                                              two or three
And was going to the Big House for a life of misery.
He nearly went stir crazy, but he got a stroke of luck.
They brought in bad George Raft for stealing liquor
                                                              off a truck.
And when some creep got mad with him, it was
                                                     Jimmy saved his life
Taking on the kitchen con who always had the knife.
So George promised Jimmy he'd do his best to see
That in the by and by, they'd both of them be free.
And when he broke his own way out, shooting
                                                          down a guard,
He still remembered Jimmy, holding him in
                                                          high regard.

George had loused up most of life, but tried hard
                                                              not to fail
When it came to friendship. He remembered Jimmy
                                                               in jail.

Life Class

And when the proof had come his way, he did the best
    he could.
He broke back into jail to see the evidence come
    good.
So Jimmy's name was cleared and all the papers
    shouted
That Jimmy was a hero, and the Bad Guys had been
    routed.
But George had got to stay in jail, there was no hope
    for him.
His only satisfaction – he had saved his buddy Jim.

Strange how real life shadows the shadows on
    the screen!
Jimmy went into politics when the Mob was real
    and mean.
They plotted to kill brave Jimmy, the Actors'
    President,
To drop a giant lamp on him and claim an accident.
Jimmy was gonna take the fall, they'd got him in
    the frame.
Fighting studio corruption was an unhealthy
    kinda game.
This time when it happened, everyone would see
He was going down to Hell for the likes of you
    and me.
But George was at a party and when he *heard* of it, he
Buttonholed his gangster pals Bugsy Siegel and
    Frank Nitti.
"I grew up with this guy, you guys," he told
    the criminal crew,
"and nobody ices him – not even guys like you."
Oh, how they moaned and muttered! But tough
    George got his way
And Jimmy got to live his life and the Mob had
    lost the day.
That's how Jimmy beat the Mob and all the
    papers shouted
That Jimmy was a hero, the Union hoods were routed.

Life Class

George stayed out of the headlines, boozing and
                                                shooting craps,
He kept his own sweet part of it strictly under wraps.
It happened many years ago, but Now It Can Be Told!
The story behind the story after the cameras rolled.
Jimmy and George grew very old but stayed the
                                                best of friends
While the movie fans of yesteryear lost interest
                                                in their ends.
For George had loused up most of life, but tried
                                                hard not to fail
When it came to friendship. Other principles
                                                might pale.
When his fame and fortune faded away along with
                                                his greasy hair,
He bought his toupees off the peg. People wondered
                                                who would care?
And when he died, he died alone, there was no joy
                                                for him.
But his one true salvation was: he had saved
                                              his buddy Jim.

An Episode of Dr Who

In the lake the sword has naturally tarnished.
Too much time under water,
too little lubrication at the hands of the squires,
too much head-breaking, heart-thrusting, blood-letting
by the late Arthur,
our rightful lord.

On the field the skulls are buried.
Too many daisies and dock leaves,
too much horse dung and dogshit,
too many matchstick towers, jerry-built
by the Saxons,
our natural replacements.

In the sky a surprising clearness,
an egg-blue loveliness,
a cloudless culmination,
as though nothing had happened,
no civilisation like ours kick-started into the dark.

Extract from the Minutes of the Monthly Meeting of the General Council of the Commune of Arras at 1830 hours on 6 Messidor, 1793

Because:
The Officer of Judgements
has been observed to be careless
at cleaning his blade
with each operation,
in the heat of summer
the square is unhealthy
and measures must be taken
swiftly in this matter.

Therefore:
The Officer shall be obliged
to clean the blade
every time he carries out
an operation
by throwing water from an oak bucket
and rubbing with a linen kerchief,
both specially provided,
and washing the ground around.

Furthermore:
The General Council,
being mindful of the closeness
of the instrument and the crowd,
commands a basket or baskets
be made and lined with oil-cloth
so transport may be performed
with dignity and efficiency,
as is done in Paris.

This resolution carried unanimously by show of
                                                    hands.

Family

I called my dad last night.
He came round just before ten,
covered in mould and grave muck.
I said: "You've heard about mother?"
He answered with a nod.
Death had not made him talkative.

I tried again.
"But you've not *seen* her yet?"
This time he laughed.
It *was* a daft question.
There's no light underground,
not even in daytime.

Eventually he shook his head.
"I thought to find her with *you*, son."
Oh, come on, dad!
It took nine months and nerve to dig *you* up.
"Three days," I told him,
"is no time at all for resurrection."

He was still smoking Capstan Strong
though I'd told him it was a health risk
and I'd have to open all the windows.
"The way she treated you… " I started.
He said: "You always shift the blame."
I thought: *I always shift the blame.*

He stubbed his fag on the
kitchen Formica. "Be a man,"
he said, "but do it in your own time.
Eternity's too bloody short."
Then he got up and left by the back,
careful not to frighten the neighbourhood dogs.

So I think I'll have mom round
next weekend. I've set some time

aside. We could sink a bottle
of Burgundy, an old trick
of ours so we don't have to talk much.
Death changes nothing, does it?

A Famous Five Afternoon

It was a Famous Five afternoon
that lasted all summer till the gypsies left.
Father was locked in his study again
with ten of the world's top scientists.

So thank Goodness the weather was fine for a picnic
and Mother had packed a whole fruit cake
for Anne and Timmy and Julian and Dick
and George (that's short for Georgina).

A ship with a yellow and purple flag
sent semaphore signals to Pebble Beach.
But Uncle Quentin, who had a hot temper,
saw it all and twice phoned the police.

So thank Goodness the water was fine for a swim
and Mother had washed enough towels
for Anne and Timmy and Julian and Dick
and George (that's short for Georgina).

For librarians lurked in dark alleys of the heart,
determined to suck out the syrup of childhood,
knowing for certain the future was theirs,
that the Famous Five would have to grow up.

So thank Goodness somebody wrote it down,
someone who knew that summer's too short
for Anne and Timmy and Julian and Dick
and especially short for Georgina.

The Farmer's Song

At the corner of the year,
at the turning of the work,
to know that you're someone
and to let the others know,
you go to the show.

To see your neighbours' faces,
and to watch their eyes
as they watch their words
as they see how things go,
you're there at the show.

Talk grows warm from the kindling of memories,
as the day folds up in the shoulder of the dark.

Everything measured,
labelled first, second, third;
and every soul judged.
To live here and grow,
you go to the show.

The Farmer's Wife's Song

The men don't come since we can't pay the rate
and it's longer hours for *him,*
though he doesn't say much about it.

And he's had to do the extra
since we bought top field from the Harpers.
We got it cheap when they moved away
when we worked out we needed the land.
He doesn't say much about it,
he doesn't say much about anything.

It's seven pence a pint from the milk
and we know we can't live on that.
We're a loss leader now, the superstore says.

But he doesn't say much about it.
He doesn't say much about anything much.
It's one of the habits he's losing.

But I see the way it's taking him
at the dead end of the day
with a glass or two and a fall into bed
and I do the cleaning and I watch TV.

One thing about having my boarders,
my bed and breakfast folk,
I don't mind taking their orders,
it's the one chance I get to talk.

He doesn't do much of a night now.
He doesn't do much of anything much.
He doesn't do much and I understand.
I'm one of the habits he's losing.

Fidelman Revisited

After Bernard Malamud

The picture completes *itself*.
It assumes a wholeness: the man and the
                              woman together,
a hint of fear in her eyes, the tightness in his gut
cleverly suggested by the dark lines in the neck.
The mystery revealed in paint.

'The picture is a marvel,' says Esmeralda,
'you've caught me as I am.'
And she kisses him.

But what would *she* know?

Ludovico says: 'Of course, the picture is a marvel.
You've caught the strangeness of her beauty
- what does it matter
if you've made yourself a tad too handsome?
Some will talk about Lucian Freud,
but I say you've surpassed him
in applying his techniques.
Others might say there is an excess of darkness:
a soupcon of lemon, a trace of crimson
might make the difference. But it's up to you.'

'Piss off!' says Esmeralda.
And when Ludovico leaves, they go to bed.

And in the morning he wonders what to paint next.
Maybe Ludovico with his sneaky eyes.
And he opens the curtains on the first light
and he thinks: maybe the man was right,
or at least not completely wrong.
And he takes a soupcon of lemon
a smudge of chrome yellow
a squidge of vermillion

a splash of magenta
and a whole tube of burnt sienna.

And when Esmeralda finds him,
leaning over the sink,
he has opened a vein with a sharpened palette knife:
more than a *trace* of crimson.

Fitter Than Fit

And he smiles a smile as big as an ambulance.
Though I don't know what *ambulance* is.
Or what *know* is. Or what *is* is.

And he smiles and says: 'You'll be allright.'
And I smile because I'll be allright.
Though I don't know what *allright* is.

And he smiles and says: Do you know who this is?'
And I turn my head as far as I can.

And I think: *Here I am then
in a world without words*.
Though I don't have the words to think it.

And I think: *That's strange*.
If you can think a thing is strange
without knowing *strange*.

And later, when I know *strange* again,
I find my malady is really a culture:
I have joined a tribe.
I did not have a *fit* but a *seizure*.
I am not an *epileptic* but a *person who has epilepsy*.

And the people who tell me this,
I think they're strange.
Now I remember what *strange* is.

Friend David

FLICKER go the lights. "Last orders please!"
He buys a round of lager and
returns, holds the tray up with his knees,
removes the glasses with his one free hand
(I help him all I can) and takes the empties back.
I rearrange the beermats, losing track
of previous conversation. I make
some effort and politely slake
a vanished thirst in sips.
Finally he says:
"Hey, do you know what's wrong with me?"
I say I couldn't guess, but yes,
please tell. The beer is cold on my lips
and reminds me of reality.
I almost decide to make a joke
(a charm to ward off philosophy).
He says: "Now I'm the sort of bloke
who can't make up his mind.
I want your advice. Should I go or stay?
Sometimes I think I should get away
and leave all this behind.
Can you say? What would *you* do?"
I decide to take the long-term view
as I fumble for my glass,
that perhaps, and then again, we'll see
- and though I'm playing, I pass.

O DAVID who has been a friend to me, his friend,
must see the ritual to its end.
Bats, I think as I piss in the yard,
live hard;
transmitting sound
only to rebound.

Godchild

SLOWLY, in wonder at itself, the stubby arm
                                          reaches out,
the sausage fingers spread on the face of the deep.
A cry guttural - and there is light.
A snort nasal - and the darkness separates.
A giggle. A glug. *Googoogoo*.

Thinks. In the beginning is the thinks.
and a finger in the gummy mouth,
and in the ages following,
in the days before counting,
in the thinks before words,
everything:
everything playful,
everything surprising
everything willed and wilful.

Before the days of counting,
before the thoughts that *have* to be words,
before commandments, decrees and punishments,

before the endless feeds and stomach pain
                                      and sore wet places,
before teeth,
before teething,
before a tooth for a tooth,
there is such a moment:
I am that I am.
I am not yet what I have done.

Such a moment!
A thinks. A thinks about mischief.
A giggle. A glug. *Googoogoo*.

Hairless in Gaza

I LOST my hair at 25,
strand by strand
then hand over hand.
I vilified God,
calling Him all sorts of names
not normally connected
with such as the Almighty.

God called me back.
'What's all this?
Didn't I give you
blue eyes,
an aquiline nose,
hair all over your *chest* at least?

'Nobody's perfect,
not even Me,
though you might have heard otherwise.
Didn't I do
my best for you,
slaving over a hot primeval soup?'
He paused for breath.

'And another thing!
What about people with *real* problems,
like lepers and lunatics,
bastards with boils,
or the paranormally paranoid?
And the Armenian Massacre
and the Black Death
and the Cripples of Calcutta,
to name but three
alphabetically?'

I hung up on God,
drank a beer and whisky chaser,
seriously unconvinced.

Then I met a girl with long legs
and interesting pointy breasts
who liked bald men.

And I got religion again.

Handbag

They found her still warm after the attack,
Or cardiac arrest, as the coroner put it afterwards.

The stolen handbag was quickly discovered
And the suspect detained within days.

The court heard a small amount of cash and
No real evidence of force,
Not enough to imperil the rest of us.

And the boy with the fingerprints wore a Live8
                                                               T-shirt
And did nothing to upset the jury.

And when he got home, his mum told the press
He was just a lovable rogue and she wouldn't have it
                                                        any other way.

The House

Stone cannot see, but stone absorbs
and changes through the chemical reaction
with water, air, people.
So I who am stone have changed as you
                          have changed.

My infancy was Church Latin and chain mail,
when you shared me with the animals.
Now, after a thousand years, you share me
                          with machines.
Sheep, goats, hens and hawks
all give way to electric points.

I was gentrified in Georgian times,
my ribcage splinted with oak beams,
the timber taken from ships,
so I grew used to the taste of sea salt.

When you grew tired of water from the well,
you invaded me with cast iron pipes
so rivers flowed through my new arteries,
full of peat and red worms.

One of you to win back his wife
turned my cowshed and loft
into kitchen and bathroom
to no avail.
A good house is the setting for love
but not its source.

It is hard to know surgery from assault.
When a Heinkel exploded in the field above
it tore my roof with fuselage and bullets.
And when you new-lined my chimney
you took away twelve barrowloads
of soot and jackdaw nests
that I had grown fond of.

Where do you end and I begin?
When clawfoot bath gives way to jacuzzi,
outside squatters to inside flush,
turf and heather thatch to slate and insulation,
herringbone stone to brick and plasterboard,
then I will be changed and so will you.

Humans see and humans absorb
and change through chemical reaction
with water, air and stone.
But you and I shall not be fossilised.

Hover on the Wing

Taste of blood is a scary thing,
Stop dead in tracks, hover on the wing,
Listen for the sound, no such thing,
Stop dead in tracks, hover on the wing.

Smell of you gone, the goodbye thing,
Ground fall away, no birds sing,
Cold, cold sweat and wasp sting,
Stop dead in tracks, hover on the wing.

I don't know why you been so long
All you left is this one-note song
I don't know why you been so long
I only know - no, no! - you gone.

Telephone tomorrow, no bell ring,
No more you, whatever else it bring,
Head start sweat and hands start wring,
Stop dead in tracks, hover on the wing.

The Incomer's Song

The hills have eyes - sheep's eyes.
Like emeralds in sunlight,
like cats' eyes they glitter
when the sheep lie heaped like candyfloss
on a sizzling road at Fryup End.

I moved here for the walking.
did my leg in after three weeks.
Now I'm happy just to be talking,
happy in heat to be watching
my life go by like the sheep.

The people here are friendly enough,
always ask about my leg,
always wave from their four-by-fours
as they try to get round the sheep,
punching their horns and swearing.

They've always lived here, you see,
but an incomer still has the vision,
has a tourist's eye for the greenness,
the grass, the trees, the moss on the bank,
the gleaming eyes of the sheep.

Jigsaw

*(To photographer Richard Billingham who won fame
depicting his grotesque family)*

His mother and the jigsaw - and his mother
                                                      a jigsaw too,
Liz sat back in her flower print dress with her arms
                                                      a tattooed blue.
Father on the sofa *sans* National Health front teeth,
Oh, Ray's a laugh, the funniest man to come out of
                                                      Cradley Heath!

Life Class

And faceless Jason, Playstationing for 30 hours
                                            or more,
ratcheted down from Druggie High, to twitch upon
                                            the floor.

And this to come home to every day. How much
                              might be *too* much?
No friends, no talk, no trust, no sex, no company,
                                            no touch.
But his room was well lit and full of books - so the
                                  Council let him be,
and he read and worked and drew things that nobody
                                            would see.
And he went away and came back again and nothing
                                      seemed to change
but the world had made its mark on him and his soul
                                      was rearranged.

And the joke of the Instamatic was it took so long
                                            to show,
to make a bit of a difference, to put his mind on go.
Now his monsters stare from the walls of the world,
                              his nightmares cut a dash
and it doesn't seem to matter that he always used
                                      built-in flash.
The ugliness he would never deny has broken away
                                      from his mind,
leaving him living and well enough, lone survivor
                                      of his kind.

Ketchup

(A lexicographer encounters the dying.)

A splodge of red at the corner of his mouth turns
                                          out to be
not blood
but the remnant
(*a surviving trace*)
of the egg and chips with ketchup
(also *catch-up, catsup,* through Malay from Chinese)
he'd been given for lunch
(from Spanish, *lonja,* a slice of ham).

'Did you like it?' I shout.
My father's wild eyes search the universe
                                       for inspiration
his mouth puckers and frets
his legs stiffen and tremble
his arms circle his head.
Then he scratches his bald patch
(*hairless, bare, without restraint,* same root as *bold*)
and he smiles the tight bright smile of
                                       showing willing.

But we both know he is playing the old man's game
of making time expand.

'He finished every bit,' says the nurse, not too proud
                                       to help him out.
The very lilt of her
(Middle English *lulte,* origin unknown)
announces her to be a cheerful body.

'Yee-ee-s,' he manages, and grins without teeth.
The nurse says: 'There!'
(*in that space, at that point,* interjection expressing
                                       reassurance, finality)
and fits them over his gums, explaining:

'They had to go for washing.'
(Old English *wascan*, Old High German *wascan*,
                              same root as *water*).

The nurse goes away. We are absurdly alone
(*single, solitary, by oneself, unique*)
except for the beds in a row
and Sheryl Crow on the radio
and the sweet sick smell of shit and disinfectant
and Sheryl Crow on the radio
and the man in the corner,
older even than my father,
lost with his toast
crying out for marmalade
(French *marmelade*, Portuguese *marmelade* from
                              marmelo, a quince)
because he doesn't like Marmite
(late English trade name from the French for *pot*
                              or *kettle*).

And Sheryl Crow on the radio:
A Change Would Do You Good.

And I get home. And my second wife Ruth
(*pity, remorse*, Hebrew through Middle English)
with the same name as my first
(who simply walked out on a midsummer's
                              morn leaving me Ruthless)
says: 'I know it's depressing
(*pressing down, letting down, causing to sink,
                              to humble*)
with him the way he is, with his mind gone
(*passed from one place to another*)
but for him it's company
(*any assembly of persons or beasts or birds*).
Anyway, it can't be for long.'

And I think: 'For *how* long?'
And I think: 'O Father

(Old English *fader*, German *vater*, Latin *pater*)
who art in hospital,
thy death be done
quickly, quietly
for the sake of thine only son
(*male child, offspring, issue*, same root as *father*).'

Laura in the Evening

SHE suddenly exclaims how real
the plastic fruit is in the alcove, lit
by pink electric light
with waxen branches sprouting out from it.
I nod. The waiter pours the coffee and I feel
a stodgy satisfaction with the night
- the theatre, meal
and coffee (white).
Mints come sickly
as talk turns quickly
to religion and the arts,
Pope John XXIII and Joyce.
She never finished Ulysses but liked its parts.
She is, of course, a Catholic by choice.

The Left Side of My Brain

That right hand belongs to me.
I can feel it with the left side of my brain,
make the thumb stand up to say I'm OK,
make the finger point to another cup of tea.

My legs, you see, ran out on me,
so I swopped them for the wheels,
had my arse traded in for a plastic bag
plugged into my navel surreptitiously.

Some people ask *Is he OK?*
and some people tell me I'm fine,
so I grin and engage my good left brain
to make it a right thumb time.

That right hand belongs to me,
it cradles the left hand protectively,
it's got used to living precariously
out the left side of my brain, like me.

Leonardo

He's a maniac, says the pretty
Girl in blue ski-pants. *No,
I'm not*, I say. *Yes*, she says,
Then: *No. It's not you.
I meant him*. I look
Across at Leonardo.

He stands tall but pretty,
Almost a girl in the face but
Broad shoulder and hard belly.
(*Biceps like steel cables*
Is a phrase I once read
But can't remember where.)

He's a maniac, she says again, and
I say: *Yes, he is!* And I
Laugh and she laughs too
And looks at him as though he
Fills the room. And I grin and know
I will never be Leonardo.

Life Class

My wife says OK:
if you *have* to do a class,
if you *have* to improve yourself,
why don't you paint still life -
apples and pears and the occasional banana?

I say:
fruit has its limitations
in revealing the eternal truths of humanity.

She says:
how come they never have *male* models?
How come it's always
the *men* doing the looking
and the painting
and the going-on about eternal truths?

I say:
I'm sure she has a point
but the reasons are probably historical.
And when I have it framed
and bring it home,
she makes me hang it in the garage.

There's only room
for *one* naked woman
in *our* bedroom,
she says.

Limestone Pavement

("A hundred-metre vertical pure limestone precipice is clearly seen from a distance to Malham Cove" - Arthur Gemmell, Malhamdale Footpaths and Bridleways, 1975)

Here is the ancient remnant of our nervous start,
of the cooling of the liquid earth that let us in with
                                                      a chance,
though briefly. Here is the dead heart
of giants whose molten movement started *our* dance.
Even the eggy sun now fails to ignite the life of rock.

More ancient than the life of grass and tree,
for whom the friendly wind still manipulates captivity
to provide the illusion of motion,
the sole communion of stone is with ocean
as old
and cold
as itself, seeping through pores, drilling and chiselling
                                                    scar and pock.

I think of Frankenstein the sculptor, pursued to
                                                    the Pole,
final judgement pending.
After hot clay and formless hope, he came to this
                                                    icy ending.

Little John: A Political Memoir

I've always hated Little John. The
Name, I mean. *Little* is my
Family name, and *John* my parents called
Me. It was Robin turned it
Round. For a laugh. For a
Joke. He made them laugh
At me. So they made *him*
Chief instead of me, you see.

Who beat him at staves? Answer
Me that! Stood on the
Footbridge, cudgelled him and gave
Him a wetting in the weir? That
Wiped the smile off for a
While. His face turned Lincoln
Green. And they still made *him*
Chief, not me, you see.

And who was the better bowman
then? Don't laugh else I'll
smack your head. I've split his
arrow oftentimes. I've had grown
men all of a-quiver. *Him* hit
gold? He couldn't piss up a wall on a
moonlit night. But they made *him*
chief, not me, you see.

I recall our confab at the Boar's
Head. We signed the parchment over
Mead and venison-in-a-basket.
'You're still a young man,' he said, 'I'll
see you get your chance.' *Fat* chance! It's
all because of the name. *Big* John
they'd've voted for! That's why, you see,
they made *him* chief, not me!

Love a la Carte

In the restaurant of the hungry heart,
where the barman measures out time of day
along with whisky sour
and a cocktail stick is *de rigeur*
in the lobe of the ear during happy hour,
there will I plight my troth,
mon amour propre,
mon amour fou,
there will I order a life for two.

Where the menu is printed in Times Dun Roman
and the daubers in the toilet use joined-up writing,
I will ensure I leave an adequate tip
equivalent at least to the wages of sin,
and take an all-inclusive trip
across the desserts
to my just deserts,
mon amour fou,
mon deja vu.

Oh, I will return, I will dissemble.
I will become those things I only now resemble.

In the bedroom, sickroom, of the hungry heart
where the linen is changed once a week
along with my prescription,
I will engage the nurse in conversation,
I will exercise my power of description.
I will say - oh! - *that* and *this*.
It will not be judged amiss.
But in all of this I only seek to woo
an aftertaste of you.

Love Strikes

The pale disease of love
has made me over in monochrome.
I have had to deny the rainbow,
the footlights of Monsieur Degas,
the fiery head of Vincent,
and even glorious Technicolor. ®
And I can't even claim the alibi of surprise.
The warning came up in a window as always:
my brain had performed an illegal operation
and was about to be closed down.
And all I could do was click OK.
And all I could do was click OK.
So be sure you're willing to provide compensation,
a suitable prize for the competition,
consolation for all my trouble,
O troublesome one.

Love's Consolation

In the desperate clockwork of these days
what chance is there to form the unknown word?
Time stutters and its mumble dies away,
the gestures comical, the rhetoric unheard.
Street names confuse me; I turn away and find
scant comfort in this disconnected factory, my mind.

Yet your touch still amazes me. It catches unaware
the quick in me as I habitually demand
the feel of your belly breathing there,
the breast and puckered forehead and
                                      comfortable hand.

But repetition breeds this dread: you might resent
the indulgent ceremony when novelty is spent.
Only believe you are all of this conceit:
my salvation from perpetual defeat.

The Maddest Thing

'The maddest thing a man may do in this life is to let himself die just like that, without anybody killing him, but just cut off by his own melancholy.'
                         - - Don Quixote by Miguel Cervantes

A book may save you when a woman fails;
when the prim and proper smell of it primes your
                         lust for words,
for the long adventure of the paragraph;
when, open and naked, it lies in wait for you,
such innocent rows of sentences leading shamelessly
to the climax on the final page.
Oh, a book may help you be a man.

A thought may save you when a friend fails;
when the hint of memory inflames emotion,
burns a hole in your solitude, some rough reminder;
when a sudden insight shows kinship with
                         cold planets
swimming in the neighbourhood of galaxies;
when eternity settles the heart as aspirin settles
                         the head.
Oh, a thought may help you stay alive.

For the maddest thing a man may do is die for reason,
cut off by a taste for logic;
and the best and boldest thing is to live for no
                         reason at all,
delaying a death for the hell of it.

Midsummer Nightmare

WHEN the Midsummer evening comes down,
                                   comes down,
like a pretty cousin on a visit,
I wear my yellow socks and lace my old suede shoes.
I show her round the town on any old excuse
and forget the big brown dog.

When the Midsummer evening goes down,
                                   goes down,
like ice cream with lemon soda,
it leaves bubbles in my glass
but they very quickly pass,
leaving a reflection of the big brown dog.

For the Midsummer evening that shoots through
                                   like a breeze
is a tease.
With breathless ease,
it wraps you in its linen and takes you to its bed.
It capers and cavorts till you forget to hold your head
and the night comes out in spots like a disease.

So take care, beware the Midsummer evening.
Put twilight from your mind.
For the Midsummer evening promises, promises,
but the big brown dog walks behind.

Mostly Unaffected

I am mostly unaffected
by wild purple flowers,
being a home-town brown-site boy;
by pale stars and splurging sunsets,
being a confirmed user of electric light;
by the high seas of the heart,
being an emotional landlubber;
by community,
being a loner;
by family,
being nobody's child and certainly nobody's cousin;
by drugs,
being an Aspirin-twice-a-day man;
by drink,
being too often sober;
and by religion,
being on first-name terms with God.
(Hello, Lord!)

But do not think me so arrogant
as to be unaffected by *you*, my love.

That would be a sad day for both of us.

Mystery Play

Death is no mystery. It's
What we had at the
Beginning, but forgot. We
Suddenly plunged into daylight, then
Thought of nothing else. Now
We catch ourselves dimming
Ever so much, a little here,
A little there, and half
Remember it.
Life, we realise, was oh-so
Strange, something machines and
Rocks never had, altogether
Too fanciful for us to
Take in at the time. Now the
Sudden sickening feeling: we
Know we should have been
More – what's the word? –
Appreciative. That's it.

The Naming Game

A tale about In-comers

I say to Tom - he's my husband -
they're in again, those people,
buying firelighters and frozen food,
getting barbecue sets.
They want the Gazette delivered,
they give me their name and number.
I've written number in book,
I'm not so bothered with name.

Names take time, you grow into names.
Too soon for that, my Tom says.

The say my wife sent them over
and he asks me to look at his Volvo,

there's some trouble with his petrol flow.
He talks to me about Manchester
about where he used to live.
And I say it must've been nice.
And I check the cheque and the signature
but I don't bother reading the name.

Names take time, you grow into names.
Too soon for that, the wife says.

I see them in pub of a Friday
He calls out hello and I nod.
And I turn back to the lads I'm out with.
I don't make any big show of it,
not wanting to cause offence.
I only want to get on wi' things.
He don't know my name, not yet,
and I've forgot about his.

Names take time, you grow into names.
Too soon for that, the lads say.

The Neat Goodbye

Let the red curtain drop.
Let the pricked ears be glued.
Let the brain and eye divorce
                          amicably.
Let the great fireproof cliché come down.

And in the aftermath
let there be a healthy lack of meaning
vigorous emptiness
no need of form
nor justification.

And let there be a coolness
like evening
and a dryness

like the oven after baking
but with no scent remaining
to recall the bread.

Novelty

Here you go again, looking for novelty:
a spot of foreign travel,
an out-of-body experience,
fresh perfume for the lobes of your ears.

So see as much of the world as you can.

There you go again, thinking words matter,
listening to the ends of your sentences,
watching yourself in the mirror,
staring at me from under screwed-up eyelids.

So leave me here as long as you will.

And don't come whining back.
And don't come *crying* back.
And don't come *gushing* back
as if it isn't important.

But see you *come* back.

Number

The word is made flesh
but the *number* becomes electric.

In bleeps and blips
fits and starts
it talks to me
on the shortwave of the synapses
wooing me with its romance
with the broad sweep of its power
turning equations into smart bombs
key strokes into caresses
provoking a passion
but defeating my grasp of the language,
like an old Edith Piaf record

when I drop the needle oh so gently,
and crouch, and listen too intently.

One Day He Pushed the Dinner Plate Away

One day he pushed the dinner plate away,
Said: "I won't be watched
Across the tablecloth, under the
Duvet, getting fat, growing
Old, getting drunk, going bald."
He said: "I'll do those things
All by myself in future,
When the only eyes are ignorant eyes
Of faithful dog and flattering cat."

She was shaken but silent. They
Agreed to separate.

One day she took the photo
Out of the sideboard, stuck it
Upright on the telly,

Said: "I was told he'd had turns but
I didn't know the half. Now I
Find his neighbours took him
Soup and filter-tip cigarettes.
And when they asked, he told them
He'd always lived on his own."

After that she was silent. Her
Solicitor handled probate.

One day the children buried her,
Said: "She had plenty of chances but
No-one else came near to him." The priest
Said: "I do know living alone isn't
Easy for people and swans."
They nibbled at turkey and hand-carved ham,
Sipped Breakfast Tea and Boddingtons,
Looked round at themselves getting fat, growing
Old, getting drunk, going bald,

And started in silence to contemplate
That pushing away of the dinner plate.

Pet Names

I call you angel but you'll never be a saint:
I wouldn't want a woman like that.
I wouldn't know what to do.

You smack me on the mouth
and I go to the bathroom and I wash away the
                                      blood and...
it's not so bad,
it's a taste I've got used to,
a woman kind of thing.

Where there are pockets of light
on the dark of the stairs,

you stand inside them,
not quite beckoning
but available.
Now there's a comfort.

I call you angel but you'll never fly.
Sometimes I think
I'm the one who holds you down.

Peter the Pathfinder

In his green and blue
wagon, shooting through
like mercury in a capillary,
Peter the Pathfinder
invades the arteries of the countryside.

He sizes situations
and parks with panache.

He reads the readers
and the readers read him:
the teacher with a taste for sex and shopping,
the brigadier with a bent for biography,
the wife with a wish to walk
on the wild side of the moors.

In his blue and green
chariot of dreams
like Mercury hang-gliding from Olympus,
Peter the Timelord
relays the stories of ten thousand years.

The books he dispenses
are lotions and lozenges
to the headsore and heartsick,
salves and seltzers
to the anxious and the out-of-sorts,

uppers and downers
to the depressed and demonic,
valid in the valleys where even Vodaphones fail.

Down the spiral staircase road to Beckhole,
in the narrows of Nab End,
on the open way to wherever,
off the shelf but never off the wall,
he decants his celebrity passengers:

Herodotus and Herriot,
Tony and Jessica Blair,
Frank Meadow Sutcliffe and Tractors in Technicolor,
military memoirs and murders most popular,
end even weighs the wants of western fans:

Gunfight in Tombstone,
Ambush in Abilene,
Showdown in Very Large Print.

The Planting of the Penny Hedge

(Commissioned for the first Caedmon literary festival in Whitby)

THE GULL-SHRIEKS are a lullaby.
They soothe me in the attic of this small hotel
smelling the fish smells
smelling the seaweed
tasting salt in the air.
The gulls reassure me that the world rolls on,
that the sea rolls on.

I have no desire to be a tourist.
I never carry a camera.
It is the mark of a stranger
searching for the picturesque.

"Oh, I hate girlie things," says the girl,
"like skirts.
But I love my skates
cos grinding is mint.
And I hate the grass cos it ruins my skates.
And I don't like the skate park with only one ramp.
Oh, they say they'll build a sports centre now
but they said it before my dad was a man,
before he worked the trawlers.
Now he works in Birmingham."

And they have planted the Penny Hedge again,
a prickly sight, sparse hair on Abraham's Bosom.
It must withstand three tides
as all of us withstand three tides:
the past, the present and the future.

In the past is the legend:
the murder of the hermit by the huntsmen,
the act of penance,
the strong stakes pared by the penny knife,
the solemn making of the first hedge.

Life Class

Three tides, three murderous gentry.
But if the stakes withstand the sea,
then the sinners are forgiven.

In the past is the legend.
The Captain of the Tides:
three tides, three voyages, a new map of the world.
Whitby was his school
and his lessons navigation, mathematics
and the insides of coal ships.
For a coal ship would take him
to the end of the world
and the end of his life.

In the past is the legend:
even the fisherman.
Three tides, three moods:
heart set upon the sea and its freedom,
mind set against the sea and its might,
bodies accepting the sea and its majesty.
For our lives are awash, the sea is everywhere,
the gulls its singers and familiars.

THE GULL-SHRIEKS wake me for the day
more reliable than the alarm call.
They rouse me from my duvet in this small hotel
smelling the bacon and decaffeinated coffee.
The gulls reassure me that the world rolls on
past breakfast time.

I never wanted to be a tourist
but sometimes it comes to that:
a suspicion I might
be searching for the picturesque.

"I love my bed," says the boy,
"it's comfy.
But I hate my sister cos she bosses me about.
And I hate all the world and vegetables.

Life Class

*And I hate things creeping up on me.
And I want to live in a desert
with sands like here but nobody about.
And my mom and dad are getting a divorce
since he went to work in Birmingham."*

They have planted the Penny Hedge again
but in the present sown seeds of doubt.
The National Debunking Society
have published a detailed report
doubting all intelligence
from any distant planet
like the Planet Earth eight centuries ago.

Hedge-planting, they say, was a compulsory service
rendered by users of the Abbot's coalyard
and it has only become symbolic
through a failure of memory.

The Captain of Tides, they say,
molested natives, lost good crew
and hardly discovered anything
that wasn't known before
or was due to be discovered anyway.
And his poor wife had to bring up all the children.

And the fishermen, they say,
just caught too many fish.
But the Ministry of Fisheries has put paid to that
with fleet capacity reduction targets,
so that should be allright then.
As long as the gulls don't catch too many.

THE GULL-SHRIEKS wake me for my final day,
and I walk down to the Esk,
past the shop with Sutcliffe's sepia pictures
of naked boys and overdressed girls,
past the windows of jet jewellery,
past the vampire postcards,

passing up my chance of the White Rabbit Trail.
I find the Astra, load my case into the boot.
The gulls are sorry to see me go.

*"I still come here for the sea," says the man,
"all the way from Birmingham.
The sea takes me out of myself."
But the woman says: "It's a serious sea"
(she said it as she was leaving me)
"...and you shouldn't use it for therapy."*

And I know I've become a tourist
and all of us are tourists now,
revisiting our history,
searching for the picturesque.

But I'm glad they've planted the Penny Hedge.
I'm glad they decided to brave three more tides.
For if the stakes withstand the sea,
then past and present are forgiven,
and there *will* be legend again.

Poet's Summer

It was Poet's Summer: shimmering heat
mirrored up from the white dust floor
of the pub car park at Lythe,
(griddled feet demanding a full half-hour
under the cold tap afterwards)
and the sun a Belisha beacon
over Crocodile's Head at Sandsend.

It was Poet's Summer, some may recall:
blazing days, a few showers overall.

It was Indian Summer: some exotic
monsoon coming down at high noon,
paddling pools where once were puddles,
a big beck up at Littlebeck;
wet tops down at Bank Bottom;
and at Cow Wath and White Hart as well,
the washing away of washing lines.

It was Poet's Summer, some may complain:
cloud like cowpats and driving rain.

It was Poet's Summer: I was out on the road,
seeing what traffic was going my way,
on the lookout for rhymes and signs of the times
(like *Ferrets for Sale - Hardworking Parents*
and a transit labelled *Van Gough)*
and making notes to work on at night
to render it all in viable verse.

It was Poet's Summer, some may have heard,
but the weather remains and outlives the word.

Police Presence

Yes, say the police, we are aware
of a number of complaints:
a shooting, a rape, some aggravated burglary
                                               and theft,
the burning down of a small number of houses,
many of them derelict.

We have discussed the situation
with community leaders and architects.
We have invited disabled pensioners
to a coffee morning with PC Steve.
We have set up a neighbourhood forum
in partnership with Europe.

And we will soon be touring the schools
with a constable dressed as a pig
(PC Steve again)
to win young people's hearts and minds.

For now, we advise people in general
to conceal any valuables unobtrusively about
                                               their person,
to always remove the steering wheel after parking,
and to walk quite slowly down the middle of the road
while keeping an eye on the traffic.

We advise all shopkeepers to bank their takings
at least twice a day
and follow a new route each time.
And, of course, we advise all women
not to wear short skirts.

But that's just common sense.

Portrait of the Artist

Every picture tells a story, Joe,
but you put the pig in the pigment.

Nothing prepared me for *you*.
Not your busty mini-skirt mother.
Not your fatty little brother.
Not your screechy denim sisters (surprisingly thin).
Not even your pictures: jagged purple lines and yellow
                                                    squares.

I stand in your fat sweaty shadow.
I shake your fat sweaty hand.
I gaze in your sweaty bread pudding face
topped by a scribble of hair all… *sweaty.*
I politely sip my Chardonnay and say:
"Tell me about your pictures…"

Now your sweatered belly heaves.
Your breath breaks out in a wheeze.
You say: "I couldn't tell you. They just come."
After a pause for more breath and belly:
 "It's like somebody else inside me. Like God."

(I nod.
Not like sweat then.)

"That one over there," you say,
 "I was pretty sick when I painted that. Medication."
You tap your nose conspiratorially.
And I start to say: "Yes, I can see that."
Because I certainly can.
But you don't wait to hear me, Joe.
You suddenly turn and walk away.
And talk to your screechy sister.

So goodbye yellow brick squares.
So much for my brush with art.

Preparations

A poem for Advent

She scrubbed the floor of the nursery
though bending was hard, her belly so big.

She dusted the tops of wardrobes
and the fruit at the bottom of the bowl.

She stood on chairs to wash windows
until she got dizzy and lay on the bed.

She played CDs of whale sounds
until the neighbours took umbrage.

She collected small bottles of vitamins
until Joseph said she could open a shop,
then she dragged him along to a video
on the joys of being a dad.

When the letter came from the government,
she packed the overnight bag,
studied the times of trains
and cheap day tickets to Bethlehem.

She realised now it would never go as planned
and she allowed herself a sad little sigh.

Prepared to Make a Statement

You took your time bringing me in,
And no mistake.
But now I say
To show there's no hard feelings:
Well done, lads.

You'll remember my note.
'Stop me before
I kill again.' And
I've done three since then.
But you know that, lads.

And there's still my day in court.
Or weeks, I shouldn't wonder.
Something to look forward to
For all of us.

Well, what do you think?
Names in the papers. Sends
Little shivers. But
You've earned it, you lot.
Well done, lads.

Psalms and Proverbs

We was never looking for trouble.
We obeyed the lord and walked in his laws.
We didn't cause no trouble.
Let the field be joyful and all that is therein.
But they always pick on us.
O sing unto the lord a new song.

We was minding our business.
I will behave myself wisely in a perfect way.
But he kept looking at our Zoe, that's what she said.
A good woman is priced above rubies.
And I just went over and had a word.
O sing unto the lord a new song.

And then it all got iffy.
Let the sea roar and the fulness thereof.
But it wasn't my fault. He was well out of order.
I will walk within my house with a perfect heart.
And I never saw nobody kick him.
O sing unto the Lord a new song.

In fact, I'm pretty choked what they done to him.
When I said my foot slippeth, thy mercy held me up.
It must've been an accident whoever it was.
I will set no wicked thing before mine eyes.
And I'm not saying nothing till my social worker
                                    gets here.
*O sing unto the lord a new song. Enter his gates with
            thanksgiving and his courts with praise.*

Rear View Mirror

From the canalside
you can see the backside
of other people's lives.
Skimming the surface,
not breaking the skin,
you give them no whim
to be startled,
to jump down,
turn around,
to put up their goodside,
sunnyside.

Here are the factories
pallet-piled,
rust-encrust,
high-wire fenced.

Here are the houses
brick-backed,
concrete-yarded,
rubble-rounded.

Here are the grass banks
rubbish-strewn,
litter-louted,
brown balding.

Here are we, no offence,
looking and loitering
on the browngreen water,
backing up,
passing by.

The Reception

When your wife re-marries
Being very modern
She invites you to the service
And to the buffet afterwards.

When you get the invitation
Being very modern
You *repondez-si-vous-plait*
Look forward to the buffet afterwards.

And at the buffet you drink:
One Cognac and ginger ale
One sherry Amontillado
One pint of Stella
Two pints of Tetley's and a Johnnie Walker chaser
And one vodka Martini

For you have been shaken
And wish to be stirred.

And when your wife's re-married
Being very modern
You stand in line to kiss the bride
And then you punch the groom.

And you feel some satisfaction
In the buffeting afterwards.

Rhymers

How should he write of their coming together?
Should he start with the time of year, the weather?
Perhaps he should say
in his straightforward way:
when the cold nights drew down
love came to town.

How comical and warm
when viewed above the storm
are scenes involving parts
somewhat lower than their hearts,
as, tangled in the bedclothes wild,
they acted Christmas and the greedy child.

But in the name of honesty
he had to make her see
it could have been anyone probably,
just a matter of geography.
Picking up the rules of the game,
she acknowledged much the same.

He wondered if tendering tenderness
was only the sign of a kind of duress.
Was it perhaps the undress rehearsal
for a thing universal?
Or merely love's action aped in spite
to get the look of emotions right?

He had trained himself to remain unaware
of change, deceit and all his share
of the little things that always go wrong.
And though he sang more than his usual song,
one day in new sunshine she went away
for he could not make his end-rhyme: *Stay.*

The Risks of Love

ASHES cover the pathway to the door of
                               managers' minds.
Their souls need to take out policies.
They only glance at the morning through blinds
                               drawn high in the sky.
And the risks of love are menaces.

Bankers' wives only want it hedged by securities,
guaranteed twelve months against normal wear
                               and tear,
Eng Lit students are pleased to join sororities
and have visiting professors accidentally touch
                               their hair.

But the risks of love have no traffic with precedent,
solicitors do not find them in manuals of reference.
They ride away in taxis, inconsistent and incontinent
and spill into your lap without the slightest deference.

Shocking Memories

Oh, I've a shocking memory now…

I was a sister in a hospital.
I looked after babies and old folk.
With both of them, it's always the same.
You end up wiping their bottoms.
In the end, I'd rather have babies.

Forty-one years in the army.
And I made lots of friends, I did.
I wouldn't have missed it, oh no.
And even now I'm on standby.
But I don't think they'll call me up again.

I've worked hard all of my life.
Never married, though I've known some men.
Once I looked after children.
Now I keep a couple of cats.
Cats are OK. They don't turn on you.

I was a sailor like my father.
I went all over the world:
Argentina, Albania, Africa.
But I remember when I was a kid
playing on Tate Hill Beach.

I started work in a grocer's shop.
They sent me out on deliveries.
I had a basket in front of the bike.
Those days I was always on time.
These days I wonder where all the time went.

Oh, we've a shocking memory now…
Can't tell them from us.
Babies and soldiers.
Sailors and cats.
Those days we were always ourselves.
These days we wonder where all the selves went.

Showstopper

I daren't stay longer, I mun go
to be up yonder at the show.
Every year it's my ambition
to win outright each competition.
Some may favour that blue faced Leicester,
but I've reared one I know'll best her!
Three or four beetroots long and pointed?
I've grown carrots double jointed.
Six hen's eggs may be opened by judges?

Life Class

I can get double yolks from my budgie's.
Champion Himalayan adult rabbit?
I know the bunny that'll grab it!
Five round potatoes, coloured or white?
Mine have got eyes - oh, what a sight!
And what about stationary engine (steam)?
My engine's the stillest you've ever seen.
Decorated horse - in any gears?
Best handwriting - under eight years?
Jar of chutney - extra mature?
Biggest thistle from horse manure?
Four white or brown or wholemeal buns?
Fastest filly in best of three runs?
Baked egg custard in shortcrust case?
Anything made out of bobbin lace?
Any ply of knitted mittens?
Any trio of playful kittens?
Hand-carved walking stick or crutch?
Best decorated gerbil hutch?
Shepherd's crook all in one piece?
Pair of check trousers without a crease?
Best six legs, handler and dog?
Best four eyes, farmer and hog?
Four fat rascals on a plate?
Ten green bottles in a crate?
Any soft toy, knitted or crotchet?
Ey up now, I'd better watch it.

I don't want to win it *all*, y'know.
They might not let me into next year's show.

Sins of the Fathers

I WAS lying low in Gaza thinking about Absalom,
hoping my father wouldn't sacrifice me,
when a personal caress
made my fingertips digress
but my conscience wouldn't let me be.

I was walking out of church ignoring the collection,
staring at the priest who was staring back at me,
when some man I might have saved
was hounded to his grave,
and my conscience wouldn't let me be.

I was hiding in a sewer underneath the motorway,
waiting for a funeral to pass by over me.
The hearses never came.
(The horses had gone lame
or the traffic was to blame.)
Now things can never be the same.

Now my conscience won't ever let me be.

Skeletons

If the surfaces of life do not talk,
how is it we are spoken to?
We have only the surfaces for clues
about our love for each other.

If the skin of you is untrue,
who is to know the difference?
So do not disabuse me yet.
Give me time to enjoy things as they seem.

And when it comes to revelation,
to the head-cracking, eye-watering crunch,
I will know I have got the skin thing wrong,

that surfaces often lie.

So ease me down to reality with your usual smile.
I give credence to a glimpse of teeth as I wait
                                            for the bite.

Skunk Tale

This is the law of the skunk:
if it *can* stink, it *will* stink.

She put them to bed. She read them *The Cat in*
                                          the Hat.
I put *you* to bed. I read your secrets with
                                        my fingertips.
She played kids while you and I played grown-ups.

She says Joely has a cold and Adam a new tooth.
I say sorry I was late, sorry for missing *The Cat*
                                        in the Hat.
I say the software crashed and we went into back-up.
I say it took two hours.

I see her nose wrinkle. From skunk.

Some of Us Make Ourselves Sick with Hope

Some of us make ourselves sick with hope
Watch ourselves hating, hate
Ourselves thinking, think
Ourselves winning eventually
Something – surely – better than this.

Some of us weep and wander and mope
But make ourselves ever sick with hope.

Some of us make ourselves sick with hope
Tap the dial of the digital watch, watch
Old lovers through alcohol minds, mind
What we're saying, always pretending
It matters to anyone much.

Some of us drink and others take dope
But either way we stay sick with hope.

Some of us make ourselves sick with hope,
Dream we've succeeded, succeed
In believing, believe when there's only
The shadow of morning reminding
Us all of the nature of night.

Some of us even at end of rope
Make ourselves ever sick with hope.

Soulmates

Intelligent opinionated down-to-earth girl
                      seeks similar fun-loving boy.
Superman sought by sensual Scorpio for
                          unusual spiritual joy.
N/S tall F with GSOH would LTM ex-boy scout,
view to spending quiet nights in and also fun
                                nights out.
20-something M seeks 38D blonde, into yoga, aerobics
and squash.
Grant Mitchell look-alike, own car and teeth, likes real
ale and home-made nosh.
House owner, professional, sporty and black
lost your first message - please call me back.
Heart for sale, two previous owners,
no whingers or lefties or losers or moaners.
Compassionate F, enjoys good wine,
seeks veggie for f/ship - and more, given time.

In the neatest of columns, with warnings besides
- don't give out your address, don't accept rides -
Genuine of Jarrow and Solvent of Surrey
check out the numbers, their hearts in a flurry.
But what is the r/ship between hoping and hype?
Can a lifetime's desire speak in seven-point type?
Though love and its like are always free-wheeling,
trading trust for lust, and groping not feeling,
I long for Slim But Soulful to score with United Fan
and Minnie the Minx to soothe the hurt of
                             real-life Desperate Dan.

The Stephen Joseph Theatre Restaurant

In the wide window
blinking in sunshine
caught in its spotlight
we are displayed to the street below.
We make a different stage of it,
munching on Mustard & Coriander Sausages
and what the menu calls
The *Restaurant's* Salmon Fishcakes.
(How could they *not* be the Restaurant's?
Someone would need to smuggle them in.)

And Stephan Grapelli plays... something,
Gershwin or Porter, but hardly heard
above consonants and teacups.

And the waitress takes my order too intently
and at tip-time is tip-toe breathless with her thanks,
as though still auditioning for the part.

I choose tomato and basil for my side dish,
but life itself is a side order here.
And I wonder if food writers take it all seriously
like their drama critic colleagues,
pocketing the menu as a souvenir?

Sunset at Helenopolis

St Helena was the mother of the emperor Constantine, who made Christianity the official religion of the Roman empire. Constantine married Fausta, who then had a passionate affair with Crispus, his son by another woman. Constantine had both of them killed. Helena, who had adored Crispus, found a new purpose in life – discovering the whereabouts of the True Cross on which Jesus was crucified. She reportedly succeeded in this, even finding the nails, which she had made up as a bit in a horse's bridle and sent to Constantine as a gift. Constantine finally created a retirement home for his mother in a town which he named Helenopolis.

The locals call it *Whore*-opolis.
They think I don't know, but
Really I don't mind.
A whore is how I started
And I finish in a town
That's named after me.
And I have to say: *I'm satisfied*.

The legionnaires call me Little Mother,
But then I've always liked soldiers.
Like me, they don't expect much,
They take life as it comes.
What came to *me* was a son,
Ruler of the world, king of kings.
I'd be a fool not to be satisfied.

And my son had a son who was laughter in my life.
And my son had a wife, a bigger whore than me.
And everybody knows what wife and son did
In the Roman afternoons.
And everybody knows what *he* did to them,
My son, the king of kings,
Quite properly in the circumstance.

The Bishops are planning to call me a saint,
But I say: *It's a bit late for that.*

Enough that I found their cross for them,
Enough that I found the nails
And sent them hammered in a bridle
To my son, the king of kings,
To rein him in when he won't be satisfied.

And I dream of Christ calling out
To his father made of sterner stuff.
For *his* father also knew law and custom –
Far beyond our Roman afternoons.
And I need to ask this father:
Was *his* son the laughter in *his* life?
On that I need to be satisfied.

Survivors

There was this nuclear holocaust or something.
And only two survivors, you and me,
washed up on this island
with lots of ripe fruit and healthy salads
and a modest dry white hidden deep in a very
                                            cool cave
and a small generator to power the CD player
and all the Harry Potter books.

And I'd always fancied *you*

But after a while you started a gang.
All by yourself.
And you went hunting crabs
and leaving your footprints on my washing.
You said: *For some people, pineapples are never*
                                                enough.
And I really felt out of it.

And then you raided my camp
and scratched my Sting and my Ella Fitzgerald
and I said: *Right. That's it!*

But there's nowhere to go and no-one to go with.

So now I say: *Let's make up.*
And I'll try to like crabmeat.

Tellyland

It did actually happen that a tourist in Goathland, North Yorkshire, asked me the way to the pub and I didn't twig that he meant the one in the Heartbeat TV series. That started me thinking about how the people there have to live, as it were, on the set of a TV show

This fella asked me the way to the pub
and I pointed him out the nearest one.
No, no, he said, the Aidensfield Arms,
cos he wanted Gina the barmaid.
I said: Well, we all want Gina the barmaid.

But I don't like living in Tellyland,
supping my pint in somebody else's life.

Family come up from Bradford,
said how broke up they'd been
when that nice Dr Kate went and died.
But they don't blame Nick for marrying Jo.
And I said: Well, neither did I.

But I don't like living in Tellyland,
going to people's funerals when they've only
                              changed their jobs.

And yet… and yet…

I dream about having a speaking part
and all the words on the auto-cue
so I don't dry up and sound like a prat,

and close-ups and make-up cleverly done
so I know I won't look sweaty or fat.
And folk then must needs listen
and folk then must needs watch,
not giving me interruption
not walking into my shot.
Now wouldn't that be nice for once?

Woman told me the other week
she'd offered to move in as housemaid
to Claud Jeremiah Greengrass
but the bugger didn't even reply.
And I said: there's a few turned quite snooty
                                      these days,
and the worst is Alfred the dog.

So I sort of like living in Tellyland,
cos sometimes you can sort of switch off.

Those Wayward Boys

Here's an ode to the wayward boys,
Tom Sawyers, Just Williams, Bertie Woosters and all
bursting with a certain *je ne sais quoi*
good *garcons* to have when your back's to the wall.

Here's to the age before girlies - ugh!
Here's to Huck Finn and *Stand By Me*.
No fear of foolishly falling out,
no chance of confusing available with free.

Here's to the days before jobs - amen!
- before post and position, pause and poise,
before those shades of a *des res* house
begin to close upon wayward boys!

Travelogue

Don't talk to me of foreign places
- Rome or Crete or Katmandu.
The only parts that interest me
are soft, warm secret parts of you.
For if I had a million pounds,
I'd fly to you so soon,
not on these wings of poesy
but in my jetplane - zoom!
I'd span the nervous oceans
and plummet from the sky.
I'd stretch you out like a lazy cat
and into you I'd fly.
And lo! beneath the crumpled sheet,
Rome and Katmandu and Crete!

A Trick Worth Knowing

Love is always a lesson,
a training in taste:
a learned affection for colouring of hair
for a strangely angled view of belly and breast,
for some rude accent delivered in extremity.

Love is always a growing up,
a sideways glance at limitation,
of damage done,
a getting-used-to,
that manages to look like novelty.

Love is always a trick worth knowing.

Voices of War

I:
<u>The Traveller's Bar</u>

It's been a tricky day
But I've turned a trick myself.
Spend well to end well
Make your mark or get marked
Take it as it comes
Another day got through.

Big hand on the three
Little hand somewhere else
My eyes move without me telling them
Middle afternoon in middle England
Take it as it comes
Another hour got through.

Allah Akbar, Allah Akbar
Ali in the Traveller's Bar
All glass and glasses
Chrome and cocktails
Sunlight, summer dresses
Show the breasts of young women
Ali in the Traveller's Bar
Sipping orange
Waiting
That's him. That's me.

All the people looking for something
Meaning of life and stuff
Blue-peaked caps and big black Uzis
Looking for me. I sit here like
I've all the time in the world
All the people in the world to get through.

II:
Voice of the Prophet 1

Kurt Vonnegut told his children:
'Never rejoice in the massacre of your enemies.'

But hear me, hear me,
Hiroshima,
Sixty years after,

I am glad it was you
Not me.

I am glad your children
Not mine.

Not quite rejoicing then.

III:
Cold comfort

God, how I hate Romantics!
Hate how they love everybody
Usually to death,
Leaving no doubt
They are radical, revolutionary,
Too damn high to tie down.

Give me a Tory Nuke 'em Newcon
Regular respectable
Hater of humankind
Sitting in his loft, window curtained,
Bountiful of bile and
Restricted in his view.

Give me boundaries, not vistas,
Graffiti-splattered
High-rise blocks that make a proper
Backdrop of the sky. Give me
Hemmed-in, crabbed, confined and focused
Like little creature-of-the-hedgerows me.

IV:
Voice of the Prophet 2

The day the IRA checked out,
the front of the Daily Telegraph said:
"The cost of peace in Ulster" and listed:
3,637 killed, 45,000 wounded, 15,300 bombs, 36,000
shootings, 300,000 troops.

I did a quick tally and made it
42, the meaning of life.

V:
Overview

Look. The sky is an envelope, it
Wraps our heads and hands and feet in
Violent blue. We knew
All along the land was an illusion
And the ocean a special effect.
There are no divisions in the universe
Only the infinite sky is real
And the horror is to take it all in.

My thoughts like marshmallow
Were too long moulded
In sweetness, grown pulpy
Like the fruit of an elongated summer. Now

They ripen in a different season,
Made to erupt and suppurate,
React to reality like skin-rash.

VI:
Voice of the Prophet 3

George Orwell said:
"The quickest way to end a war is to lose it."

So I'll not be praying for peace then
Nor tolerance nor understanding
Nor brotherly nor sisterly love
Nor forgiveness.

No. Certainly not forgiveness.

I'll pray for victory:
Absolute irrevocable unarguable
Like death which is
Its other name.

Wagonwheel

It was 1915, Valentine's Day,
I was out delivering churns.
And the wheel come off me wagon.
And I was browned off, bloody knackered,
milk all over the road.
And bloody's a word I never used in the house.

I went home and told me mum.
'I've had enough. I've signed up.
I'm off to go to war!'
'You're a bloody fool,' she shouted,
tears all over her face.
And bloody's a word she never used with us kids.

I was 18 months in the trenches.
I was losing lots of friends.
Their legs come off, their heads come off.
I was bloody scared. Bloody right.
Blood all over the place.
Bloody's a word I'd long got used to by then.

Now I pop in the pub on Poppy Day,
and somebody stands me a drink.
They know I was bloody lucky
and they're hoping a bit rubs off.

'Bitter? Not half,' I say,
'You can get me a Bloody Mary if you've got the
Worcester sauce.'

Oh, these days I've got *all* the wheels on me wagon.

The War of the Worlds

Chapter One: The Attack on the World Trade Center

The towers are falling in slow motion.
Not the endless replay on Sky and Digital
Not the last fierce moment for the firemen on the
                                              ground
Not each night's unfolding nightmares of family and
                                               lovers.

The 757 like an insect
Its bite breaking out in septic flame
This was the last of the action.
The rest is routine, long naming of the dead, the
                                       formaldehyde of waiting.

But the towers are falling in slow motion
Now their shadows stretch beyond anything the sun
                                               has made
Now their weight grows heavier than engineers could
                                               calculate
Now the dust billows like an apron in the oven's blast
Wafts over oceans, mimicking a shroud.

To be continued...

We've Not Had Much of a Summer So far

        Pale summer, cool summer,
    real summer's anaemic young cousin,
      the underweight undergraduate,
   Elizabeth Barrett-Browning of a season,
  your image strained through stained glass,
        I will have to live with you
         a little white while then
          until the real thing,
        the bright brass ring thing
        yellow woman summer,
         naked sun summer,
           fat, fleshy,
        immodest, immense,
          pudding-hot
            summer
          comes along.

What

What of love then?
It may be passionate yet long to make its peace.
It may be fierce yet find a quiet goal.
It may be wide as galaxies yet lie in the space between your breasts.
It may burn bright as comets yet become the placid ocean.

And what of the *loss* of love?
It is the loss of all these things,
of time and space, self and other.

My love, let me not lose you.
For what of either of us then?

Wired

She's full of wires, says her mum
On the phone. And straightaway
I picture it, well, *think* I do.
She may have said something…
Tests. Doctors. Feeling really tired.
Only not *operation*.
Only not *wires*.
I'd've remembered that.

We're waiting on results, says her mum
And straightaway I know.
How furtive quick she always was – is –
Was before the *wires* at least,
Avoiding cracks on pavements. In
The beginning isn't always the word,
Well, not the word *wires*.
I'd've remembered that.

Give her my love, I say to her mum,
But it doesn't sound like love, it sounds like fear.
I'm another avoider of cracks.
And her mum says: *Didn't I actually*
Meet you once, late
And raining at the bus station?
And I say: *yes*. And at last I make a smiley sound.
I remember *that*.

Woof and Warp

Woof, woof, says the big black hound behind the
                                             gates.
Woof, woof, I say, being a dog lover.
Woof, woof, it says, very loud, and bounds along
                                             behind its fence,
loping parallel with my direction.
Ey up, I say, *I'm not there yet, come back.*
Woof, woof, it says, returning, responding well (I
                    think) to our little game,
then bounds off behind the fence again.
Silly, I say, *woof, woof, I'm back here, you dog you*!
It comes back apologetically and wags its tail.
Ahh. Peace in heaven.

"Ey up," says a voice
 as a bobble-hatted head pokes up above the fence,
"You're winding up my dog!"

"Winding up your dog?" I say,
"I get off my bus
and I'm walking down my street,
and I'm just being friendly,
and I'm paying back barks with the language of
                                             Shakespeare,
swopping amity for enmity,
and getting, I think,
an educated response.
Until *you* turn up."

Ashamed, I think, he slides down behind his fence.
"Come back, Mr Baskerville!" I shout,
but he thinks better of it.
He knows who is leader of the pack.

A victory for common sense then.

Later, when I go to post a letter,

I make a point of passing the gate again
with some shaggy doggy patter prepared.
But the big black hound has gone.

Not punished on *my* account, I hope.

Words

Words is
only words is
only words
I tell myself
as I compose concertos
that come out honky-tonk.

Now my day skulks indoors by the gas fire.
When it behaves like this, I pay it no heed.
I tell myself the day is a liar:
it would have me write
by electric light
but I open a brochure and read.

No reason to go where others have led.
No reason to crawl when they fly.
Even while putting myself to bed
I am bound to say
I give nothing away
not even how my

words is
today.

www.ingramcontent.com/pod-product-compliance
Lightning Source LLC
Chambersburg PA
CBHW022108160426
43198CB00008B/391